Navigating Your Mental Health:

Embrace the Journey

By

Georgina Twumasi

ISBN: 978-1-955312-96-7

Printed in the United States of America

Story Corner Publishing & Consulting, Inc.

Chesapeake, VA 23321

Storycornerpublishing@yahoo.com

www.StoryCornerPublishing.com

Table of Contents

Introduction

Mental health is a crucial aspect of overall well-being, encompassing our emotional, psychological, and social states. For teens, navigating mental health can be particularly challenging and overwhelming due to the many changes and pressures they face during adolescence. Whether you're dealing with depression, anxiety, bipolar disorder, ADHD, or another condition, understanding how to manage and support your mental health is essential for leading a fulfilling life.

This workbook is designed to help you understand more about the emotions and thoughts you're experiencing and to show you that you are not alone. You matter, and your mental health is worth nurturing. In this book there are both education and practical exercises to help teens manage their mental health challenges, empowering them with tools for effective coping and seeking help when needed. It also provides resources to support you in recognizing triggers and setting goals.

We will explore various mental health challenges like depression, bipolar disorder, anxiety, and more, while also offering strategies to help you on your journey. Whether you're struggling with a diagnosis or simply want to better understand your emotions, this is your space for growth, reflection, and healing.

Purpose of This Workbook

The primary purpose of this workbook is to equip you with the knowledge and skills needed to manage your mental health proactively.

It offers:

- Education: Understanding your mental health condition and how it affects you is the first step toward managing it effectively. This workbook covers the symptoms, triggers, and impact of various mental health conditions.

- Practical Strategies: Learn about self-care, coping techniques, and communication skills that can help you navigate everyday challenges and emotional ups and downs.

- Support Resources: Discover different resources, including professional help, faith-based support, and self-help tools, that can provide additional support when needed.

- Personal Growth: Explore how goal setting, problem solving, and spiritual practices can contribute to your personal development and overall well-being.

Why Do Self-Care and Coping Strategies Matter?

Managing mental health involves more than just addressing symptoms; it requires a holistic approach that includes self-care and effective coping strategies. Self-care is about intentionally taking care of your physical, emotional, and mental well-being. It helps prevent burnout and maintains a balance between your responsibilities and your personal needs.

Coping strategies are techniques that help you manage stress and emotional challenges when they arise. These strategies are essential for handling the ups and downs of life, especially when dealing with mental health conditions. By developing and using these strategies, you can build resilience and improve your ability to cope with difficult situations.

How to Use This Workbook

This workbook is divided into several sections, each focusing on a different aspect of managing mental health. You can work through the sections in order or focus on specific areas that are most relevant to you. Here's how to use it effectively:

1. Reflect: Take time to reflect on each section and consider how the concepts apply to your own experiences. Personal

reflection helps deepen your understanding and enhances the effectiveness of the strategies.

2. Practice: Apply the strategies and techniques provided in each section to your daily life. Practice regularly to build habits that support your mental health.

3. Seek Support: Use the resources and support options outlined in the workbook to find additional help when needed. Don't hesitate to reach out for professional support, join support groups, or connect with others who understand your experiences.

4. Adjust as Needed: Your mental health journey is unique, and what works for one person may not work for another. Feel free to adjust the strategies and techniques to suit your needs and preferences.

A Path Forward

Embarking on a journey to manage your mental health is a courageous and important step. This workbook is here to support you every step of the way, providing guidance, resources, and encouragement. Remember, you are not alone on this journey, and there are many tools and people available to help you.

By taking proactive steps to understand and manage your mental health, you are investing in your future well-being and happiness. Embrace this journey with hope and determination, knowing that with each step, you are building a stronger, healthier version of yourself.

Chapter 1:

Understanding Mental Health

Mental health plays a vital role in every aspect of our lives. It affects how we think, feel, and act, shaping how we handle stress, relate to others, and make decisions. For teens, mental health can be especially important since this stage of life comes with a lot of changes—physically, emotionally, and socially. Understanding mental health, how it impacts you, and what challenges can arise is the first step in building a strong foundation for a healthier, more balanced life.

What Is Mental Health?

Mental health refers to your emotional, psychological, and social well-being. It influences how you handle stress, connect with others, and navigate the ups and downs of daily life. Just like physical health, your mental health can change over time and needs attention and care to stay strong.

It's essential to understand that having struggles with your mental health is not a weakness or a personal failure. Everyone experiences difficulties at some point, and mental health challenges are a normal part of life.

Here are key components of mental health:

Emotional Health:

-This involves understanding and managing your emotions. When you're emotionally healthy, you're able to handle both positive and negative emotions and express them in appropriate ways.

Psychological Health:

-Psychological health is about how your mind works—your thoughts, beliefs, and how you process information. It's important to cultivate positive thinking patterns and challenge negative beliefs.

Social Well-being:

-Social well-being focuses on how you interact with others, the quality of your relationships, and your ability to build supportive connections.

Why Mental Health Matters for Teens

Teen years are often marked by rapid growth and change—mentally, emotionally, and physically. During this time, many teens face new pressures from school, friendships, family, and even social media. Understanding mental health during this period is critical because:

It Impacts Your Daily Life:

-Your mental health affects how well you can focus in school, how you handle stress, and how you manage relationships with friends and family. Good mental health helps you enjoy life and cope with challenges in a more effective way.

It Shapes Your Future:

-How you handle your mental health now sets the stage for your future well-being. Developing coping skills and emotional resilience during your teen years will help you better manage stress and challenges as you transition into adulthood.

Mental Health Challenges Are Common:

-Mental health struggles are common among teens and recognizing that you're not alone is important. Whether it's dealing with stress, anxiety, depression, or another mental health issue, it's essential to know that there is help available and that many people face similar challenges.

Common Mental Health Conditions in Teens

Let's take a closer look at some common mental health conditions that affect teens. Understanding these conditions can help you recognize when you or someone else might need help.

Depression

Depression is more than just feeling sad or going through a rough patch. It's a serious mental health condition that affects your mood, thoughts, and energy levels. For teens, depression can often be mistaken for normal teenage mood swings, but when the sadness doesn't go away and starts to interfere with daily life, it's a sign that something more is going on.

What is Depression?

Depression is a condition that can make you feel persistently sad, hopeless, and uninterested in activities. It's more than just feeling sad; it's an ongoing challenge that impacts your mood and energy levels.

How It Affects You: You might feel like nothing matters, have difficulty concentrating, or even struggle to find the energy to do daily activities.

Symptoms of Depression:

-Persistent sadness or feeling "empty"

-Loss of interest in activities you used to enjoy

-Difficulty concentrating or making decisions

-Changes in sleep patterns (sleeping too much or too little)

-Feelings of worthlessness or guilt

-Thoughts of self-harm or suicide

If you or someone you know is experiencing these symptoms, it's essential to seek help. Depression is treatable, and there are professionals who can provide the support needed.

Exercise: Create a "Mood Chart"

Track your daily emotions for a week. What time of day do you feel worse or best? What might contribute to these feelings?

Psychotic Depression

What is Psychotic Depression?

Psychotic depression includes typical symptoms of depression combined with hallucinations or delusions. It's a severe form of depression where reality might seem distorted.

How It Affects You: You might hear or see things that aren't there or believe things that aren't true. This can be incredibly distressing.

Exercise: Create a "Reality Check Journal"

Write down any thoughts that seem overwhelming or confusing. Next to them, write down a reality-based response. This can help separate what's real from what isn't.

Anxiety Disorders

Anxiety is a normal reaction to stress, but for some teens, it can become overwhelming and interfere with everyday life. Anxiety disorders involve constant, excessive worry or fear that doesn't go away, even when there's no real threat.

What is Anxiety?

Anxiety is characterized by persistent worry or fear about everyday situations. It can range from mild nervousness to intense panic.

How It Affects You: Anxiety can cause physical symptoms like a racing heart, difficulty breathing, and a constant sense of dread.

Symptoms of Anxiety Disorders:

-Feeling restless or on edge

 -Racing thoughts or constant worrying

 -Difficulty sleeping or concentrating

-Rapid heartbeat, sweating, or trembling

-Avoiding certain places or activities due to fear or panic

Anxiety can take many forms, including generalized anxiety disorder, social anxiety, and panic disorder. If anxiety is making it difficult for you to function, it's time to reach out for help.

Exercise: Practice "Calming Techniques"

Practice breathing exercises, progressive muscle relaxation, and grounding techniques. Write down how each one makes you feel.

ADHD (Attention-Deficit/Hyperactivity Disorder)

What is ADHD?

ADHD can make it hard to focus, sit still, or complete tasks. It affects attention, impulsiveness, and activity levels.

How It Affects You: You might find it difficult to pay attention in school, finish tasks, or stay organized.

Exercise: Do "Focus Challenges"

List 3 daily goals and break them into smaller tasks. Try a "Pomodoro technique" (25 minutes of focus, 5-minute break) to see how it helps.

Bipolar Disorder

Bipolar disorder is a condition that causes extreme mood swings. These swings include emotional highs (mania or hypomania) and lows (depression). It's important to recognize that these mood changes are more severe than typical teenage moodiness.

What is Bipolar Disorder?

Bipolar disorder involves extreme mood swings, from high-energy "manic" phases to low-energy depressive phases.

How It Affects You: During mania, you might feel invincible or overly confident, while during depression, you may feel lethargic or hopeless.

Exercise: Create a "Mood Monitor"

Create a graph to track your moods daily. Label high-energy days, low-energy days, and neutral days. Reflect on any pattern.

Borderline Personality Disorder (BPD)

What is BPD?

BPD affects how you feel about yourself and others. It can lead to intense mood swings, impulsive actions, and difficulty maintaining relationships.

How It Affects You: You might feel like you're always on an emotional rollercoaster, experiencing intense fears of abandonment, even when things seem okay.

Exercise: Create an "Emotion Tracker"

Write down the situations where your emotions felt uncontrollable. Next to each, note how you reacted and how you could have responded differently.

Chapter 2:

Self-Care and Coping Strategies

Self-care is essential for maintaining good mental health, especially when facing challenges like depression, anxiety, bipolar disorder, ADHD, or any other mental health condition. It involves taking intentional actions to care for your emotional, mental, and physical well-being. Coping strategies, on the other hand, are specific techniques that help you manage stress, regulate your emotions, and navigate difficult situations more effectively.

In this chapter, we will explore the importance of self-care, different types of coping strategies, and how you can create a personalized self-care plan that fits your needs.

Why Self-Care Matters

When you're dealing with mental health challenges, it can feel overwhelming to balance school, relationships, responsibilities, and your emotions. That's why self-care is so important—it's about giving yourself the time, space, and attention you need to recharge and maintain balance. Here are some key reasons why self-care is crucial for your well-being:

Prevention of Burnout:

-Without self-care, it's easy to feel exhausted, emotionally drained, and overwhelmed. Self-care helps prevent burnout by giving you moments to rest and recuperate.

Improved Mental Health:

-Regular self-care can help reduce symptoms of depression, anxiety, and stress. Taking time to nurture yourself can improve your mood and overall mental well-being.

Increased Resilience:

-When you practice self-care, you're better equipped to handle life's challenges. It helps you build emotional resilience, making it easier to navigate difficult moments.

Enhanced Focus and Productivity:

-Self-care helps you recharge your energy, which in turn boosts your focus and productivity. When you're well-rested and feeling good, it's easier to concentrate and get things done.

Types of Self-Care

Self-care is not just about bubble baths and relaxation—although that can be part of it! There are different types of self-care that focus on various aspects of your well-being. By incorporating multiple types of self-care into your life, you can address both your physical and emotional needs.

1. *Physical Self-Care*

Physical self-care involves taking care of your body to ensure that you feel healthy and energized. This includes basic needs like sleep, nutrition, and exercise, as well as activities that make your body feel good.

Exercise:

-Regular physical activity helps release endorphins, the "feel-good" chemicals in your brain. Exercise can also reduce stress, improve mood, and increase your energy levels. Find a form of movement you enjoy, whether it's dancing, walking, yoga, or sports.

Sleep:

-Getting enough sleep is critical for mental health. Poor sleep can worsen symptoms of depression, anxiety, and ADHD. Aim for 8–9 hours of sleep each night and establish a relaxing bedtime routine to help you unwind.

Nutrition:

-What you eat affects your mood and energy levels. Try to eat a balanced diet rich in fruits, vegetables, whole grains, and lean proteins. Avoid too much caffeine or sugar, which can cause energy crashes and mood swings.

Rest and Relaxation:

-Taking breaks and allowing your body to rest is vital. This can be as simple as spending time in nature, stretching, or taking a nap when you feel drained.

2. Emotional Self-Care

Emotional self-care involves acknowledging and understanding your emotions, allowing yourself to feel them, and finding healthy ways to express them. This type of self-care helps you process difficult feelings and prevent emotional overwhelm.

Journaling:

-Writing down your thoughts and feelings can be a powerful way to process emotions. Journaling allows you to release pent-up feelings, gain clarity on your thoughts, and reduce stress.

Talking to Someone You Trust:

-Sometimes, just talking through your feelings with a friend, family member, or therapist can help. It gives you a chance to feel heard and supported.

Mindfulness and Meditation:

-Mindfulness practices help you stay present and grounded in the moment. Simple mindfulness exercises, such as deep breathing or meditation, can help reduce anxiety and improve your emotional well-being.

Creative Expression:

-Engaging in creative activities like drawing, painting, writing poetry, or playing music can be a great way to express emotions that might be difficult to put into words.

3. Social Self-Care

Social self-care is about nurturing relationships that are positive and supportive. Having healthy social connections can reduce feelings of loneliness, provide emotional support, and improve overall well-being.

Spending Time with Loved Ones:

-Being around people who care about you can lift your spirits and help you feel connected. Whether it's talking with family, hanging out with friends, or joining a group or club, social connections are important.

Setting Boundaries:

-Healthy relationships require boundaries. Knowing when to say "no" and protecting your time and energy is a form of self-care. It's okay to prioritize yourself and take a step back when needed.

Joining a Support Group:

-Sometimes connecting with others who are going through similar challenges can be a great source of comfort. Support groups provide a safe space to share, listen, and feel understood.

4. Mental Self-Care

Mental self-care involves activities that keep your mind sharp, engaged, and focused. It's about challenging yourself intellectually and taking time to rest your mind when needed.

Learning Something New:

-Stimulating your brain by learning a new skill, reading a book, or solving puzzles can be a form of self-care. Mental challenges help keep your mind sharp and engaged.

Taking Breaks from Technology:

-Too much screen time can lead to stress, especially when you're constantly exposed to news, social media, or schoolwork. Taking regular breaks from technology helps clear your mind and reduce mental fatigue.

Practicing Gratitude:

-Taking time to reflect on what you're grateful for can shift your mindset to a more positive one. Keep a gratitude journal where you write down things you're thankful for each day, no matter how small.

5. *Spiritual Self-Care*

Spiritual self-care focuses on nurturing your spirit, finding a sense of purpose, and connecting with something greater than yourself. It can involve religious practices, meditation, or simply spending time reflecting on your values and beliefs.

Prayer or Meditation:

-Engaging in spiritual practices like prayer, meditation, or quiet reflection can provide comfort and a sense of peace.

Reading Sacred Texts or Inspirational Material:

-Reading scripture, spiritual books, or even inspirational quotes can help you connect with your beliefs and find meaning in your experiences.

Spending Time in Nature:

-Many people find a spiritual connection in nature. Taking walks outdoors, hiking, or simply sitting by a body of water can give you time to reflect and feel grounded.

Coping Strategies for Difficult Moments

While self-care is about preventing burnout and maintaining your well-being, coping strategies are tools you can use in the moment when you're feeling overwhelmed or experiencing emotional distress. Having a variety of coping strategies ready can help you manage intense emotions and stressful situations.

1. *Grounding Techniques*

Grounding techniques help you stay connected to the present moment when your mind feels overwhelmed or anxious. These strategies bring your focus back to the here and now, which can calm your body and mind.

The 5-4-3-2-1 Grounding Exercise:

-Identify 5 things you can see, 4 things you can touch, 3 things you can hear, 2 things you can smell, and 1 thing you can taste.

This brings your attention to your surroundings and distracts your mind from distressing thoughts.

Deep Breathing:

-Slow, deep breaths help activate your body's relaxation response. Try inhaling deeply for 4 seconds, holding for 4 seconds, and exhaling for 4 seconds. Repeat until you feel calmer.

2. Distraction Techniques

Sometimes, taking a break from what's stressful can be helpful. Distraction techniques offer a way to temporarily shift your focus away from negative thoughts or overwhelming emotions.

Engage in a Hobby:

-Doing something you enjoy, whether it's drawing, cooking, or playing a game, can take your mind off difficult emotions.

Physical Activity:

-Going for a walk, dancing, or exercising can help release pent-up energy and improve your mood.

Watch Something Uplifting:

-Watching a funny or uplifting video can help you feel lighter and distract your mind from stress.

3. Self-Soothing Techniques

Self-soothing involves using your senses to calm yourself down. These techniques are especially helpful when you're feeling anxious or emotionally overwhelmed.

Touch:

-Wrap yourself in a cozy blanket or hug a soft pillow. The sensation of warmth and softness can be comforting.

Smell:

-Use calming scents like lavender, vanilla, or eucalyptus. Lighting a scented candle or using essential oils can help create a soothing environment.

Sound:

-Listening to calming music, nature sounds, or a guided meditation can help calm your mind.

4. Cognitive Reframing

Cognitive reframing helps you challenge negative thoughts and replace them with more balanced or realistic ones. It's a way of shifting your mindset and breaking the cycle of negative thinking.

Identify Negative Thoughts:

-Start by recognizing when you're having a negative or unhelpful thought. Write it down if that helps.

Challenge the Thought:

-Ask yourself whether the thought is realistic. Is there evidence that contradicts it? Is it an exaggeration or worse-case scenario thinking?

Replace the Thought:

-Replace the negative thought with a more balanced or positive one. For example, if you're thinking, "I'll never get through this," replace it with "This is hard, but I've gotten through tough things before, and I can do it again."

Creating Your Own Self-Care Plan

Now that you've learned about different types of self-care and coping strategies, it's time to create your own personalized self-care plan. A self-care plan is a set of activities or practices that help you stay grounded, manage stress, and take care of yourself regularly.

Steps to Create Your Plan:

1. Identify Your Needs:

-Take a moment to think about what you need right now. Are you feeling physically drained? Emotionally overwhelmed? Socially isolated? Write down your needs in different areas of your life.

2. Choose Self-Care Activities:

-Based on your needs, select activities from each type of self-care (physical, emotional, social, mental, spiritual) that resonate with you. These should be activities that feel restorative and doable.

3. Schedule Self-Care Time:

-Incorporate your self-care activities into your daily or weekly routine. Set aside specific times for self-care to ensure you're consistently prioritizing your well-being.

4. Practice Flexibility:

-Life can be unpredictable, so it's important to be flexible with your self-care plan. Adjust your activities based on how you're feeling, and don't be afraid to try new things if something isn't working for you.

Exercise: Building a Support System

-List the people in your life who make you feel safe and supported.

- Who can you turn to in difficult times?

Exercise: Journaling & Emotional Expression

-Create a daily journal entry to reflect on your feelings, what went well, and what was challenging.

Exercise: Mindfulness & Meditation

-Practice mindful breathing for 5 minutes each morning. Write down how you feel before and after the practice.

Exercise: Physical Activity & Sleep Hygiene

-Track your sleep for one week. Are there any patterns? How does a good night's sleep impact your mood and energy levels?

Conclusion

Self-care and coping strategies are not one-size-fits-all. It's important to experiment with different techniques and find what works best for you. By incorporating self-care into your routine and using coping strategies when you need them, you're taking an active role in managing your mental health and well-being. Remember, taking care of yourself is not selfish, it's necessary for your emotional, physical, and spiritual health.

Chapter 3:

Recognizing Triggers and Symptoms

When it comes to mental health, being able to recognize what sets off your emotional or mental responses is key to understanding and managing your condition. These triggers could be situations, places, or even people that provoke intense emotions or symptoms like anxiety, sadness, or hyperactivity. Recognizing your symptoms early allows you to intervene before things become overwhelming.

What Are Triggers?

Triggers are events, situations, or stimuli that can provoke a reaction, whether emotional, mental, or physical. They can cause flare-ups in symptoms or increase feelings of distress. Triggers can vary widely from person to person, and learning to identify yours is an important step in managing your mental health.

Types of Triggers:

1. Environmental Triggers:

 -These include places, sounds, or even certain times of the day that might cause distress.

 -Example: Crowded spaces or loud noises may cause anxiety for some.

2. Emotional Triggers:

 -Strong emotions like anger, sadness, or frustration can often exacerbate symptoms.

 -Example: A fight with a friend or feeling left out might trigger feelings of depression or anxiety.

3. Situational Triggers:

 -Specific events or situations like tests, family gatherings, or social interactions can serve as triggers.

 -Example: Public speaking may trigger anxiety for some teens, or being ignored might trigger feelings of abandonment in someone with BPD.

4. Cognitive Triggers:

 -Sometimes your own thoughts can be a trigger. Negative thinking patterns, overthinking, or intrusive thoughts may set off certain symptoms.

 -Example: Constantly worrying about failure can worsen anxiety or feelings of inadequacy.

What Are Symptoms?

Symptoms are the feelings or behaviors you experience when triggered or when your mental health condition is active. Learning to recognize early symptoms can be crucial in taking preventative action before they get worse.

Symptoms may be emotional, physical, or behavioral:

-Emotional Symptoms: These are feelings that overwhelm you, like sadness, irritability, or euphoria (in the case of mania).

-Physical Symptoms: This could include tiredness, rapid heart rate, headaches, or stomach aches that are linked to your emotional state.

-Behavioral Symptoms: Notice changes in your actions, like withdrawing from others, reckless behavior, or difficulty focusing.

Common Symptoms for Each Condition:

1. Depression:

-Persistent feelings of sadness or hopelessness.

-Loss of interest in activities you once enjoyed.

-Fatigue or low energy.

-Trouble concentrating or making decisions.

-Changes in sleep (too much or too little).

2. Psychotic Depression:

-Hallucinations (seeing or hearing things that aren't there).

-Delusions (strong beliefs that are not grounded in reality).

-Intense guilt or feelings of worthlessness.

3. Bipolar Disorder:

-Manic Symptoms: Excessive energy, impulsive decisions, feeling overly excited or euphoric, irritability, racing thoughts.

-Depressive Symptoms: Similar to those in depression (low energy, sadness, trouble concentrating).

4. Borderline Personality Disorder (BPD):

-Intense mood swings or emotional instability.

-Fear of abandonment, even in safe relationships.

-Impulsive behaviors like spending sprees, binge eating, or risky activities.

-Difficulty maintaining relationships.

5. Anxiety:

-Excessive worry or fear about everyday situations.

-Physical symptoms like racing heart, shaking, or shortness of breath.

-Panic attacks.

-Avoiding situations that make you feel anxious.

6. ADHD:

-Trouble focusing or paying attention.

-Difficulty staying organized or completing tasks.

-Impulsivity, acting without thinking.

-Restlessness or hyperactivity.

Identifying Your Triggers and Symptoms

1. Start a Trigger Journal:

-Write down situations that make you feel upset, anxious, or sad. Note what happened, how you felt, and what thoughts or physical symptoms came with it.

Example Entry:

-Situation: My friend didn't invite me to hang out.

-Feelings: I felt abandoned, sad, and angry.

-Symptoms: My heart raced, and I couldn't stop thinking about it all night.

2. Recognize Early Warning Signs:

-What are the first signs that things are starting to go wrong? For anxiety, it might be a racing heart or feeling tense. For depression, it might be losing interest in things you love.

-Catching these early signs can help you use coping skills before the symptoms get too intense.

3. Patterns in Your Symptoms:

-Over time, you may notice patterns in your triggers. Maybe anxiety always flares up during school presentations, or depression gets worse when you're isolated for too long.

- Recognizing these patterns can help you make adjustments to avoid or prepare for triggering situations.

Techniques to Identify Triggers and Symptoms

Exercise 1: Trigger Mapping

- Goal: Identify common triggers and how they affect you.

- Instructions: Draw a map or chart with your main triggers at the center. Around them, write down how these triggers make you feel and what symptoms they provoke.

Example:

-Trigger: Crowded Places

-Feeling: Overwhelmed, anxious

-Symptoms: Sweating, rapid heartbeat, dizziness, racing thoughts

Exercise 2: Symptom Timeline

- Goal: Track when and how symptoms show up.

-Instructions: Over the course of one week, track any significant emotions or symptoms you experience, noting when they occur and in what context.

Example Timeline Entry:

Monday, 10 AM – Felt anxious before math test, couldn't focus, heart racing.

Tuesday, 3 PM – Suddenly felt sad after seeing friends hang out without me.

Exercise 3: Trigger Action Plan

- Goal: Create a plan for managing triggers.

- Instructions: For each trigger, write down coping strategies or steps you can take to lessen the impact.

Example:

Trigger: Tests/Exams

Coping Strategies:

- Practice deep breathing before the test.

- Study with a friend to feel more prepared.

- Talk to the teacher if I need more help.

Coping with Triggers and Symptoms

Once you've identified your triggers and symptoms, the next step is learning how to cope with them effectively. Some strategies may include:

-Grounding Techniques: These techniques help bring you back to the present moment, especially during anxiety or panic. Try focusing on your senses (what can you see, hear, touch, taste, smell) to calm your mind.

-Deep Breathing Exercises: Practice deep breathing to calm yourself when your body feels overwhelmed.

-Positive Self-Talk: Challenge negative thoughts that may worsen your symptoms. Replace them with more balanced, realistic statements.

-Mindfulness Practices: Meditation and mindfulness exercises can help you stay grounded and reduce the intensity of emotional reactions.

-Planning for Stressful Situations: Knowing your triggers allows you to create a plan for managing them when they arise. Having a set of coping strategies ready can make a big difference.

By becoming more aware of your triggers and symptoms, you'll be better equipped to manage your mental health proactively. Understanding yourself is the first step in gaining control over your emotions and improving your overall well-being.

-**Exercise:** Write down any situations that make you feel anxious, upset, or overly excited. Identify if these are "triggers" for your mental health condition.

Chapter 4:

Healthy Communication & Boundary Setting

Healthy communication and boundary setting are essential tools for managing relationships, expressing your feelings, and protecting your mental health. When you're dealing with mental health challenges like depression, anxiety, or ADHD, being able to communicate clearly and set boundaries can help you maintain healthy, supportive relationships and reduce stress.

-**Exercise:** Write down a time when you felt overwhelmed by someone's actions. How did you respond? How can you set healthy boundaries in the future?

Why Communication Matters

Communication is how we express our thoughts, feelings, needs, and desires to others. It plays a huge role in shaping relationships, resolving conflicts, and asking for support. For teens, learning to communicate in a way that's clear and respectful is key to maintaining healthy connections with friends, family, and even teachers.

When you're struggling with mental health challenges, it can be difficult to express your emotions or needs. You might feel misunderstood or not know how to explain what you're going through. However, learning how to communicate in a healthy way can reduce feelings of isolation and help others understand how they can support you.

What Is Healthy Communication?

Healthy communication involves being clear, honest, and respectful when expressing your feelings and needs. Here are the key components:

1. Active Listening:

-This means fully focusing on what the other person is saying without interrupting or thinking about how you'll respond. It shows that you value what the other person has to say.

-*Exercise:* Practice active listening in your next conversation by maintaining eye contact, nodding to show you're engaged, and summarizing what the other person has said before responding.

2. "I" Statements:

-Instead of blaming or accusing, use "I" statements to express how you feel. This reduces the chances of the other person becoming defensive.

-*Example:* Instead of saying, "You never listen to me," say, "I feel unheard when I try to share my feelings."

3. Expressing Emotions Clearly:

-It can be hard to put feelings into words, especially if you're overwhelmed. But being specific about your emotions helps the other person understand what you're experiencing.

-*Example:* Instead of just saying, "I'm upset," you could say, "I'm feeling really anxious because I'm falling behind in school, and I don't know how to catch up."

4. Non-Verbal Communication:

-Your body language, facial expressions, and tone of voice are just as important as your words. Try to keep your body language open and approachable.

-*Exercise:* Stand in front of a mirror and practice saying a difficult message. Notice how your body language aligns with your words. Are your arms crossed? Is your voice tense? Try to relax in these areas.

5. Being Open and Honest:

-It's important to be truthful about how you feel, even if it's difficult. However, honesty should always be paired with kindness.

-Example: If you're overwhelmed by someone's constant texting, instead of ignoring them, explain that you need some space to recharge.

What Are Boundaries?

Boundaries are the limits and guidelines you set to protect your well-being. They help you define what you are comfortable with and what you aren't. For example, boundaries might involve how much time you're willing to spend with others, how much personal information you share, or how you expect to be treated.

For teens dealing with mental health issues, boundaries are crucial because they help you conserve emotional energy and prevent feelings of overwhelm. They also teach others how to treat you and respect your needs.

Why Setting Boundaries Is Important

Without boundaries, you might feel drained, overwhelmed, or even resentful toward others. Boundaries help you:

-Protect your emotional and mental health.

-Reduce feelings of stress or anxiety in relationships.

-Ensure that your needs and feelings are respected.

-Create a sense of personal control over your time, space, and energy.

Types of Boundaries

1. Emotional Boundaries:

-These protect your feelings and emotional energy. They involve limiting how much emotional support you give to others and being clear about what kind of emotional support you need.

-Example: "I appreciate that you're worried about me, but I need some time to myself to process my feelings."

2. Time Boundaries:

-These involve protecting your time and making sure you don't overcommit yourself to others at the expense of your own needs.

-Example: "I can hang out for an hour, but then I need to go home and work on my assignments."

3. Physical Boundaries:

-These include your personal space and physical touch. It's important to be clear about what you're comfortable with.

-Example: "I'm not really a hugger. Could we just fist bump instead?"

4. Mental Boundaries:

-These protect your thoughts and beliefs. It's okay to have different opinions from others, and setting boundaries means not allowing others to make you feel bad for your beliefs.

-Example: "I respect your opinion, but I see things differently, and that's okay."

5. Digital Boundaries:

-In today's world, digital boundaries are becoming increasingly important. They involve setting limits on how much time you spend online, what you're willing to share, and when you want to unplug.

-Example: "I turn off my phone at 9 PM so I can focus on relaxing before bed."

How to Set Healthy Boundaries

1. Know Your Limits:

-Before setting a boundary, it's important to know what your limits are. Think about what drains your energy or makes you feel uncomfortable.

-Exercise: Reflect on past situations where you felt overwhelmed or resentful. What limits could have been set in those moments to prevent those feelings?

2. Be Direct and Honest:

-When setting boundaries, it's important to be clear and direct. There's no need to apologize or feel guilty for having boundaries.

-Example: "I know you want to hang out more, but I need some quiet time for myself this weekend."

3. Practice Saying "No":

-It's okay to say no without explaining yourself. "No" is a complete sentence.

-Example: If someone invites you to an event but you're feeling mentally or emotionally drained, it's okay to say, "No, I won't be able to make it," without giving a reason.

4. Use "I" Statements:

-When communicating boundaries, use "I" statements to focus on your own needs rather than blaming others.

-Example: "I feel overwhelmed when I'm asked to do too many things at once. I need more time to complete my current tasks before taking on new ones."

5. Stay Calm and Consistent:

-Setting boundaries may be difficult at first, especially if the other person pushes back. Stay calm and stick to your limits. Reaffirm your boundaries if necessary.

-Example: If a friend keeps texting late at night, remind them: "I really need to turn my phone off after 10 PM to get enough sleep. Can we talk earlier in the evening?"

Exercises for Practicing Healthy Communication & Boundaries

Exercise 1: Practice Boundary-Setting Scenarios

-Goal: Prepare yourself for real-life situations where you need to set boundaries.

-Instructions: Write down 2-3 situations where you struggled to set boundaries in the past. Then, write a response you could use next time to set a clear and healthy boundary.

Example:

-Situation: A friend constantly asks for help with homework, even when I'm busy.

-Response: "I'm happy to help sometimes, but I need to focus on my own work tonight. Let's find another time when we're both free."

Exercise 2: Role-Playing with a Friend

-Goal: Practice communication skills in a safe environment.

-Instructions: Pair up with a friend or family member and role-play different situations where you need to express your feelings or set a boundary. Practice using "I" statements, being direct, and listening actively to the other person's response.

Exercise 3: Boundary Reflection Journal

-Goal: Reflect on how setting boundaries makes you feel.

-Instructions: Each time you set a boundary, write down the experience in a journal. How did the other person react? How did you feel afterward? Did it help reduce your stress or anxiety?

Dealing with Pushback on Boundaries

Sometimes, people might resist your boundaries, especially if they're used to certain behaviors from you. This doesn't mean your boundaries are wrong, it just means they need time to adjust. Here's how to handle pushback:

1. Stay Firm: Remember, your boundaries are there to protect your mental health. Even if someone doesn't agree, it's okay to stand your ground.

2. Repeat Yourself: If necessary, calmly repeat your boundary. You don't have to argue or justify it.

 -Example: "I understand you're upset, but I still need space right now."

3. End the Conversation if Needed: If someone repeatedly ignores your boundaries, it's okay to remove yourself from the situation.

 -Example: "If you keep ignoring my need for space, I'm going to leave this conversation for now."

Healthy communication and boundary setting are ongoing practices. They take time and effort to develop, but the rewards are worth it: stronger relationships, reduced stress, and a greater sense of personal control. Remember, your feelings and needs are valid, and setting boundaries is not only okay, but also necessary for your well-being.

Chapter 5:

Goal Setting & Problem Solving

Setting goals and solving problems are critical skills for navigating life's challenges, especially when you're managing mental health conditions like depression, anxiety, or ADHD. Having clear goals gives you direction, while effective problem-solving helps you overcome obstacles. Both tools can empower you to take control of your mental health journey and build resilience for the future.

The Importance of Goal Setting

Goal setting is a process that helps you decide what you want to achieve and establish steps to get there. Having goals provides you with a sense of purpose, direction, and motivation. It also gives you something to focus on, which can help counter feelings of helplessness or overwhelm, particularly when dealing with mental health challenges.

For teens, setting goals can make overwhelming tasks— like school projects, managing social relationships, or balancing personal well-being—feel more achievable by breaking them down into manageable steps.

Types of Goals

1. Short-Term Goals:

These are goals you can achieve in the near future, typically within days or weeks. They help you build momentum and confidence.

- Example: "Finish reading my book by the end of the week."

2. Long-Term Goals:

These are goals that may take months or even years to accomplish. Long-term goals require sustained effort and a plan to reach them.

-Example: "Graduate high school with good grades."

3. Process Goals:

These focus on the actions you take to achieve an outcome. They emphasize daily habits or steps.

-Example: "Spend 30 minutes a day studying math."

4. Outcome Goals:

These goals are focused on the result you want to achieve.

-Example: "Make the school basketball team."

How to Set SMART Goals

A popular method for effective goal setting is the "SMART" framework. SMART goals are specific, measurable, achievable, relevant, and time-bound. This structure helps you clarify your goals and create a plan for success.

1. Specific:

Your goal should be clear and detailed. The more specific it is, the easier it will be to create steps to achieve it.

-Example: Instead of "I want to do better in school," try "I want to improve my grade in math by one letter grade this semester."

2. Measurable:

You should be able to track your progress toward the goal.

-Example: "I will track my progress by checking my weekly math quizzes to see if I'm improving."

3. Achievable:

Your goal should be realistic based on your current abilities and resources. It's important not to set goals that are impossible to reach.

-Example: "I will aim to improve by one letter grade rather than trying to get perfect scores on every test."

4. Relevant:

Your goal should align with your personal values and what's important to you.

-Example: "Improving in math is important because I want to feel more confident and prepared for college."

5. Time-Bound:

Your goal should have a deadline to keep you accountable and motivated.

-Example: "I will work on this goal throughout the semester, aiming to improve by the time final exams come around."

Steps to Achieving Your Goals

1. Break Down Your Goals:

Large goals can feel overwhelming. Breaking them down into smaller, manageable steps makes them more achievable.

-Example: If your goal is to get more organized, you can break it down into steps like:

1. Buy a planner.

2. Write down all upcoming assignments.

3. Set reminders for due dates.

2. Create a Plan:

Outline the specific actions you'll take to reach each step of your goal. Make a timeline for each action to stay on track.

-Example: "I'll spend 15 minutes each evening organizing my assignments for the next day."

3. Track Your Progress:

Keep a journal, checklist, or app to track your progress toward your goals. Tracking keeps you motivated and helps you see how far you've come.

-Example: "I'll mark each day on my calendar when I've completed my daily study sessions."

4. Adjust When Necessary:

Life happens, and sometimes things don't go as planned. If you encounter setbacks or your priorities change, it's okay to adjust your goals.

-Example: "If I don't see improvement in my math grade by midterms, I'll talk to my teacher for extra help."

5. Celebrate Small Wins:

Celebrate your achievements, even the small ones. Rewarding yourself along the way helps maintain motivation.

-Example: "If I complete my study schedule for two weeks, I'll treat myself to a movie night with friends."

Problem-Solving: Facing Obstacles Head-On

Problems are a natural part of life, but learning how to tackle them effectively can make all the difference. Problem-solving helps you overcome barriers, whether they're related to school, relationships, or mental health.

Effective problem-solving involves identifying the problem, brainstorming solutions, and taking action. When you're feeling anxious, depressed, or overwhelmed, problems can feel like impossible challenges. However, breaking them down and approaching them step-by-step can make them more manageable.

Steps to Problem-Solving

1. Identify the Problem:

The first step in problem-solving is clearly identifying what the problem is. Sometimes, it's not as obvious as it seems. Be specific and define the problem clearly.

-Example: Instead of "I'm stressed out," try "I'm stressed because I'm falling behind on my schoolwork."

2. Brainstorm Possible Solutions:

Once you've identified the problem, come up with a list of potential solutions. Don't judge your ideas, just write them all down. Later, you can decide which solutions are the most realistic.

-Example: If the problem is falling behind in school, potential solutions might include:

  -Asking a teacher for help.

  -Creating a homework schedule.

  -Joining a study group.

  -Asking for a tutor.

3. Evaluate the Options:

   Look at the solutions you brainstormed and evaluate which ones are realistic, and which might not work. Consider what resources, time, and effort each solution requires.

-Example: "Joining a study group sounds like the best solution because I'll get extra help and motivation, but it doesn't cost any money or require too much extra time."

4. Make a Plan:

Choose the best solution and create a plan for how you'll implement it. Decide what steps you'll need to take and when you'll take them.

-Example: "I'll talk to my teacher after class tomorrow to ask about study groups, and if there aren't any available, I'll look online to see if I can start one with my classmates."

5. Take Action:

After planning, the most important step is to actually take action. Even if you're uncertain or anxious, taking small steps toward solving the problem will move you forward.

6. Reflect and Adjust:

After taking action, reflect on whether it worked. Did the solution help solve the problem, or do you need to try something else? If your first attempt doesn't work, don't get discouraged. Problem-solving is often an ongoing process.

-Example: "After a week in the study group, I still feel like I'm struggling with math. I'll try asking the teacher for one-on-one help."

Problem-Solving Skills for Mental Health Challenges

Dealing with mental health conditions like depression, anxiety, ADHD, or borderline personality disorder can make problem-solving more difficult, but also more essential. Here are some problem-solving strategies tailored to mental health challenges:

1. Depression:

-Problem: Lack of motivation to do schoolwork.

-Solution: Break tasks into smaller, more manageable steps, and reward yourself after completing each small step. If you're feeling stuck, ask for help from a teacher or friend to get started.

2. Anxiety:

-Problem: Feeling overwhelmed by an upcoming presentation.

-Solution: Practice the presentation in smaller parts. Use calming techniques like deep breathing before starting. If the anxiety is too overwhelming, ask your teacher if you can present to a smaller group first.

3. ADHD:

-Problem: Trouble focusing on homework.

-Solution: Set a timer for short intervals (10-15 minutes) and take a 5-minute break in between. Create a designated space for homework that's free from distractions.

4. Borderline Personality Disorder (BPD):

- Problem: Fear of abandonment leading to conflict in friendships.

- Solution: Practice open communication by expressing your feelings honestly but calmly. Use "I" statements and focus on building trust with clear boundaries in relationships.

Exercises for Goal Setting & Problem-Solving

Exercise 1: Goal-Setting Worksheet

-Goal: Create a specific, actionable goal using the SMART framework.

-Instructions: Choose a personal goal, then write it out using the SMART guidelines.

Example:

-Specific: I want to improve my time management.

-Measurable: I will keep a daily planner to track my tasks.

-Achievable: I'll start by organizing my assignments for the next week.

- Relevant: Managing my time better will reduce my stress.

-Time-Bound: I'll start this new routine for one month and check in after four weeks to see my progress.

Exercise 2: Problem-Solving Mind Map

-Goal: Visualize solutions for a current problem.

-Instructions: Write the problem in the center of a piece of paper. Draw lines outward to brainstorm possible solutions. For each solution, write down possible steps or obstacles. Review the map and choose the best path forward.

Exercise 3: Reflect on a Solved Problem

-Goal: Identify the steps you used to successfully solve a problem in the past.

-Instructions: Think of a problem you've solved recently, no matter how small. Write down the steps you took and reflect on how you can use those same skills to solve future problems.

Exercise 4: Personal Goals

-Write down three personal goals related to your mental health. Break them down into small steps.

By setting clear goals and developing problem-solving skills, you're building the tools to take control of your mental health and personal development. Goals give you direction, while problem-solving empowers you to overcome obstacles that arise along the way. Keep in mind, progress doesn't have to be perfect, it just needs to be consistent. You're on a journey of growth, and every small step counts!

Chapter 6:

Seeking Professional Help

While self-help tools like goal setting, problem-solving, and communication strategies are crucial for managing mental health challenges, sometimes it's essential to seek professional help. Mental health professionals can provide specialized guidance, support, and treatment that may be difficult to achieve on your own. Whether you're struggling with depression, anxiety, bipolar disorder, ADHD, or any other condition, seeking help from trained professionals can be a turning point in your journey toward wellness.

Why Professional Help Is Important

Mental health professionals, such as therapists, counselors, psychologists, and psychiatrists, are trained to understand the complexities of the mind and behavior. They can offer different forms of treatment, including therapy, medication, and coping strategies that are tailored to your unique needs.

Seeking professional help is not a sign of weakness, it's an act of courage and self-awareness. Just like you would go to a doctor for a physical illness, mental health professionals provide essential support for emotional and psychological issues. Some mental health challenges are too complex to handle alone, and professional intervention can help you regain control and improve your quality of life.

When to Seek Professional Help

Recognizing when to seek professional help can be difficult, especially if you're used to dealing with your problems on your own. However, there are clear signs that may indicate you could benefit from seeing a mental health professional:

1. Persistent Feelings of Sadness or Hopelessness:

-If you're experiencing ongoing sadness, hopelessness, or a lack of interest in activities you once enjoyed, these could be signs of depression. If these feelings last for more than two weeks, it's important to seek help.

2. Overwhelming Anxiety or Panic Attacks:

-Anxiety is a normal part of life, but if you're experiencing constant worry, fear, or panic attacks that interfere with your daily activities, professional help can provide strategies to manage your symptoms.

3. Severe Mood Swings or Emotional Instability:

-If you feel like your emotions are unpredictable, swinging from extreme highs to deep lows (as with bipolar disorder) or you struggle to regulate your emotions (as with borderline personality disorder), professional support is key to understanding and managing these shifts.

4. Difficulty Concentrating or Managing Tasks:

-If you're struggling with focus, organization, or time management (which may be symptoms of ADHD), professional guidance can offer tools and strategies to help you stay on track.

5. Harming Yourself or Suicidal Thoughts:

-If you're engaging in self-harm or having thoughts of ending your life, it's critical to reach out for help immediately. Suicidal thoughts are a serious sign that you need urgent professional intervention.

6. Difficulty Managing Relationships or Social Interactions:

-If you're finding it hard to maintain relationships, whether due to conflict, fear of abandonment, or feelings of isolation, a mental health professional can help you navigate these challenges in a healthy way.

7. Trauma or Major Life Events:

-Experiences like the death of a loved one, abuse, bullying, or significant life changes can trigger emotional distress. If you're struggling to cope with these events, therapy can provide a safe space to process your emotions.

8. Substance Abuse or Addictive Behaviors:

-If you're using drugs, alcohol, or other harmful behaviors to cope with emotions or stress, seeking professional help is essential for addressing the underlying issues and finding healthier ways to cope.

Types of Mental Health Professionals

There are several types of mental health professionals, each with different specialties and approaches to treatment.

Understanding the differences can help you decide who might be the best fit for you.

1. Therapists/Counselors:

-These professionals provide "talk therapy" (also known as counseling or psychotherapy). They help you explore your thoughts, emotions, and behaviors and offer strategies for coping with challenges. Common types of therapy include:

-Cognitive Behavioral Therapy (CBT): Focuses on identifying and changing negative thought patterns and behaviors.

-Dialectical Behavior Therapy (DBT): Often used for people with borderline personality disorder or chronic emotion regulation issues, DBT helps develop skills for managing emotions and relationships.

-Talk Therapy: Allows you to share your feelings and experiences in a non-judgmental setting.

2. Psychologists:

-Psychologists are trained to diagnose and treat mental health conditions through therapy. They may specialize in certain types of therapy or work with specific populations (such as children, teens, or those with trauma). Psychologists typically do not prescribe medication but may work closely with psychiatrists.

3. Psychiatrists:

-Psychiatrists are medical doctors who specialize in mental health. They can diagnose mental health conditions and prescribe medication, such as antidepressants, mood stabilizers, or antipsychotic medications. Psychiatrists often work in tandem with therapists or psychologists to provide a combination of medication and talk therapy.

4. Social Workers:

-Clinical social workers can provide counseling and connect you with community resources or services. They often work in schools, hospitals, or clinics and provide support for those dealing with complex life situations.

5. School Counselors:

-School counselors are trained to support students with academic, social, and emotional issues. They can provide short-term counseling and refer you to external professionals for long-term care if needed.

6. Peer Support Specialists:

-These are individuals who have personal experience with mental health challenges and have received training to provide support and guidance to others going through similar issues.

What to Expect When Seeking Help

If you've never been to a therapist or psychiatrist before, it's normal to feel nervous or unsure about what to expect. Here's a breakdown of the process to help ease any anxiety:

1. Finding the Right Professional:

-Start by asking for recommendations from trusted adults, your doctor, or your school counselor. You can also search online for mental health professionals in your area.

-Tip: Look for professionals who specialize in treating teens and have experience with your specific mental health condition (such as ADHD, depression, or anxiety).

2. The First Appointment (Initial Consultation):

-The first session is usually an introductory meeting where the therapist or psychiatrist will ask you questions to understand your background, current struggles, and what you hope to achieve in therapy.

-What to Expect: They might ask about your mental health history, family dynamics, academic or social challenges, and any symptoms you're experiencing. This is a chance for you to share what's been bothering you, but there's no pressure to reveal everything right away.

3. Establishing Goals:

-Early on, you'll work with your therapist to set goals for treatment. This could include reducing anxiety, improving mood, developing better coping skills, or learning how to manage relationships.

-Example Goal: "I want to feel less anxious in social situations and learn ways to manage panic attacks."

4. Creating a Treatment Plan:

-After understanding your needs, the mental health professional will develop a treatment plan that may include regular therapy sessions, homework assignments, or a recommendation to see a psychiatrist for medication.

5. Ongoing Therapy Sessions:

-Therapy sessions typically last 45-60 minutes and occur once a week or every other week, depending on your needs. During each session, you'll work through your challenges and learn coping strategies.

-Note: Progress in therapy can take time. Be patient with yourself and trust the process.

6. Medication (If Necessary):

-If you're seeing a psychiatrist and they recommend medication, they'll explain what the medication is for, how it works, and what side effects to watch for. Medications are often used alongside therapy to help manage symptoms.

Common Concerns About Seeking Help

It's normal to have concerns or hesitations about reaching out for professional help. Let's address some common fears:

1. "I don't want people to think I'm crazy."

-Mental health challenges are incredibly common, and seeking help doesn't mean you're "crazy." It means you're taking control of your well-being. Everyone needs help sometimes, and there's no shame in that.

2. "What if therapy doesn't work?"

-Therapy is not a quick fix. It's a process that requires effort and time. If you don't feel an immediate difference, that's okay. Keep communicating with your therapist and be open about what's working and what isn't.

3. "I can handle it on my own."

-You don't have to face mental health challenges alone. Even if you're strong, getting professional support can offer you new tools and perspectives to manage your emotions and experiences more effectively.

4. "I'm afraid of being judged."

-Therapists are trained to create a safe, non-judgmental space where you can openly share your thoughts and feelings. They're there to support you, not criticize you.

5. "What if I don't like my therapist?"

-It's important to find a therapist you feel comfortable with. If the first therapist you see doesn't feel like a good fit, it's okay to try someone else. Finding the right person can make all the difference in your therapy experience.

Taking the First Step

Taking the first step toward seeking help can feel intimidating, but it's an incredibly important act of self-care. Here are some tips for making that first step a little easier:

1. Talk to Someone You Trust:

-Share your feelings with a trusted adult—whether it's a parent, teacher, or school counselor. They can help you find a mental health professional and support you along the way.

2. Write It Down:

-If you're nervous about talking to a therapist, write down your thoughts, feelings, or questions beforehand. This can help you feel more prepared for the first session.

3. Remember You're Not Alone:

-Millions of people, including teens, seek help for their mental health every day. You are not alone on this journey.

Seeking professional help is a powerful step toward healing, growth, and well-being. Remember, your mental health is just as important as your physical health, and getting help is a sign of strength, not weakness. Don't hesitate to reach out—you deserve support and care.

Chapter 7:

Faith & Spirituality

Faith and spirituality can be powerful sources of comfort, guidance, and strength, especially when navigating mental health challenges. Many teens find that connecting with their faith or spiritual beliefs helps them cope with difficult emotions, find meaning in their struggles, and cultivate hope for the future. Whether you are part of an organized religion or have your own personal spiritual practices, integrating faith into your mental health journey can provide a sense of peace and purpose.

The Role of Faith in Mental Health

Faith, in its many forms, offers more than just a belief system—it provides a framework for understanding the world, making sense of suffering, and finding inner peace all according to God's plan and purpose for your life. When mental health challenges like depression, anxiety, or ADHD feel overwhelming, faith can serve as an anchor that helps you stay grounded. It gives you a sense of connection to something greater than yourself.

For many people, faith offers:

1. Hope:

-Faith can inspire hope, even in the darkest times. It reminds us that things can improve and that we are never truly alone in our struggles.

2. Purpose and Meaning:

-Faith helps us find meaning in our challenges and gives us a greater sense of purpose. This perspective can be especially helpful when mental health struggles feel meaningless or overwhelming.

3. Community and Support:

-Faith-based communities often provide a sense of belonging and support, where individuals can share their struggles and receive encouragement from others who share their beliefs.

4. Guidance:

-Many people turn to religious texts, prayer, meditation, or spiritual leaders for guidance when facing difficult emotions or life challenges. These practices can offer wisdom and direction during times of uncertainty.

Exploring Faith During Mental Health Struggles

Mental health challenges can sometimes strain your relationship with faith. It's normal to experience doubts, confusion, or even anger when you're going through difficult times. You might wonder why you're suffering or feel disconnected from your faith. It's important to remember that spirituality is a personal journey, and it's okay to have questions or feel unsure. Many people find that grappling with their faith during tough times ultimately deepens their understanding and strengthens their spiritual connection.

Here are some ways to explore faith as part of your mental health journey:

1. Prayer and Meditation:

-Prayer is a form of communication with God, while meditation can help quiet your mind and focus on your spiritual connection. Both practices can provide a sense of calm and reassurance during times of stress or anxiety.

-Example: You might set aside time each day to pray for strength or guidance or meditate to find inner peace.

2. Reading Sacred Texts or Spiritual Writings:

-Many people turn to religious texts, such as the Bible, Quran, or other spiritual writings, for comfort and wisdom. These texts often contain messages of hope, resilience, and encouragement that can help you navigate difficult emotions.

-Example: If you're feeling lost or overwhelmed, you might read a passage that reminds you of God's presence and love or offers a perspective on how to overcome hardship.

3. Spiritual Reflection and Journaling:

-Taking time to reflect on your faith and how it relates to your mental health can help you process your emotions and gain clarity. Writing down your thoughts, prayers, or reflections in a journal can be a powerful way to connect with your spirituality.

-Example: You might reflect on how your faith has helped you through difficult times in the past or write down prayers or affirmations that bring you comfort.

4. Engaging with a Faith Community:

-Participating in your faith community can provide you with a support network that encourages your spiritual and emotional well-being. Whether it's attending religious services, joining a youth group, or connecting with a mentor, being part of a faith community can help you feel supported and understood.

-Example: You might join a group at your church or place of worship where you can discuss your mental health challenges with others who share your faith.

The Intersection of Faith and Mental Health

Faith and mental health are not separate from one another; they often intersect and influence each other in powerful ways. For example, many religious or spiritual practices encourage positive mental health habits, such as gratitude, compassion, forgiveness, and mindfulness. By integrating these practices into your daily life, you can improve your mental well-being while deepening your faith.

Here are a few examples of how faith can support mental health:

1. Gratitude as a Spiritual Practice:

-Many religious teachings emphasize the importance of gratitude, which has been shown to improve mental health by shifting focus from negative thoughts to positive ones. Practicing gratitude can be as simple as thanking God for the blessings in your life or writing down things you're thankful for each day.

-Example: Start a gratitude journal where you list three things you're grateful for each day. Reflect on how these blessings relate to your faith.

2. Forgiveness and Letting Go of Resentment:

-Forgiveness is a central theme in many spiritual traditions. Learning to forgive others—and yourself—can reduce feelings of anger, bitterness, and resentment, which can weigh heavily on your mental health.

-Example: If you're holding onto a grudge or negative feelings toward someone, pray for the strength to forgive them, and trust that forgiveness will bring you peace.

3. Compassion and Helping Others:

-Many faiths encourage acts of kindness and service to others. By focusing on helping those in need, you can shift your perspective away from your own struggles and find meaning through compassion.

-Example: You might volunteer with a charity or faith-based organization, offering your time and energy to make a positive impact on others.

4. Mindfulness and Present-Moment Awareness:

-Mindfulness, often found in spiritual practices like prayer and meditation, involves staying present in the moment and observing your thoughts and emotions without judgment. Practicing mindfulness can reduce anxiety and help you stay grounded in your faith.

-Example: During times of stress, take a few moments to close your eyes, breathe deeply, and focus on God's presence with you in that moment.

Balancing Faith with Professional Help

While faith can be a source of strength, it's also important to recognize that mental health challenges often require professional help. Prayer, meditation, and spiritual reflection are valuable, but they don't replace the need for therapy, medication, or other professional interventions when necessary.

Faith and professional help can work together. For example, many mental health professionals are open to incorporating your spiritual beliefs into therapy, and some specialize in faith-based counseling. By combining professional help with your faith, you can create a holistic approach to mental health that addresses both your spiritual and emotional needs.

1. Faith-Based Therapy:

-Faith-based therapy integrates spiritual practices and beliefs into the therapeutic process. If your faith is a central part of your life, finding a therapist who respects and incorporates your spiritual beliefs can make the therapeutic process more meaningful.

2. Using Prayer and Meditation in Conjunction with Therapy:

-Prayer and meditation can complement therapy by helping you center yourself and stay focused on healing between sessions. You might pray for wisdom, peace, or strength before a therapy appointment, or meditate on the guidance you receive from your therapist.

3. Community Support Alongside Professional Help:

-Leaning on your faith community while receiving professional help can create a broader support system. Spiritual leaders, mentors, or friends from your faith community can provide encouragement and prayer, while your therapist helps you develop coping strategies.

Common Challenges in Faith and Mental Health

Sometimes, mental health challenges can cause you to question your faith, or vice versa. You might feel like your mental health struggles are a sign that you've failed in your faith, or you may wonder why a loving God would allow you to suffer. These are valid questions and part of a larger spiritual journey.

Here are some ways to navigate these challenges:

1. Dealing with Spiritual Doubts:

-It's normal to question your faith when you're experiencing intense emotions or hardships. Instead of seeing doubt as a sign of weakness, consider it part of your spiritual growth. You can explore your doubts with a trusted spiritual leader or mentor who can offer guidance and perspective.

-Example: If you're struggling with why you're going through a hard time, speak with a spiritual leader who can offer wisdom on finding purpose in suffering.

2. Separating Mental Health Struggles from Spiritual Failures:

-Sometimes, people mistakenly believe that mental health struggles are a result of a lack of faith. It's important to understand that mental health conditions, like depression or anxiety, are medical conditions that need treatment—just like physical illnesses.

-Example: Remind yourself that seeking therapy or medication is not a lack of faith, but a responsible step toward healing, just like going to the doctor for a physical illness.

3. Finding Meaning in Suffering:

-Many faiths teach that suffering can have a purpose, even if we don't fully understand it in the moment. Instead of viewing your struggles as meaningless, try to find ways they might lead to growth, resilience, or deeper empathy for others.

-Example: Reflect on the idea that your mental health journey might help you grow stronger and become a source of support for others who are struggling.

Exercises for Connecting Faith and Mental Health

Exercise 1: Faith-Based Affirmations

-Goal: Develop a set of affirmations based on your faith that you can turn to when you're feeling down or anxious.

-Instructions: Write down a list of affirmations that reflect your spiritual beliefs and values. These can be quotes from sacred texts, personal prayers, or spiritual truths that bring you comfort.

Example:

- "I am loved and valued by God."

- "I trust that God is guiding me through this challenge."

- "I am not alone; God is with me."

Exercise 2: Gratitude Prayer Journal

-Goal: Cultivate a sense of gratitude through prayer and journaling.

-Instructions: Each day, write a short prayer thanking God for specific blessings in your life. Reflect on how these blessings help you grow, even amidst mental health challenges.

Exercise 3: Meditation on Scripture

-Goal: Use scripture or sacred texts as a tool for mindfulness and inner peace.

-Instructions: Choose a passage from your sacred text that brings you comfort or hope. Spend a few minutes each day quietly reflecting on its meaning and how it applies to your current mental health journey.

Exercise 4: Finding Purpose Through Prayer

-Goal: Use prayer to understand life and purpose

-Instructions: Write down any comforting prayers or scriptures that help you through difficult moments.

Faith and spirituality can be powerful allies in your mental health journey. They provide hope, guidance, and a sense of meaning when you're facing challenges. By integrating your faith with professional help, you can create a balanced approach to healing that addresses both your spiritual and emotional needs. Trust in your journey, and know that you are supported by your faith, your community, and those who care about your well-being.

List of Affirmations

Who Am I In Christ?

I am forgiven. Ephesians 1:7

I am enough. 2 Corinthians 12:9-10

I am rescued. Colossians 1:13-14

I am redeemed. Romans 3:24

I am God's Masterpiece. Ephesians 2:10

I am valuable. Luke 12:6-7

I am chosen. John 15:16

I am justified. Romans 3:23-24

I am accepted. Romans 15:7

I am saved. Ephesians 2:8-9

I am courageous. Deuteronomy 31:6

I am free. Romans 8:1-2

I am wonderfully made. Psalm 139:14

I am a new creature. 2 Corinthians 5:17

I am born of God. 1 Peter 1:23

I am adopted by God. Ephesians 1:5

I am a child of God. John 1:12

I am Jesus' friend. John 15:15

I am a citizen of heaven. Philippians 3:20-21

I am a member of Christ's body. 1 Corinthians 12:2

I am never alone. Joshua 1:12

I am loved. John 3:16

Conclusion: Embracing Your Journey

As you come to the end of this workbook, you've taken a big step in understanding your mental health. It's important to remember that your journey toward mental health and well-being is ongoing. Every step you take, whether big or small, is progress. Remember, healing is a journey, and it's okay to ask for help when you need it. Keep practicing the tools you've learned here, and don't hesitate to reach out to your support system.

You've learned about the significance of recognizing triggers, communicating effectively, setting boundaries, and seeking help when necessary. You've explored goal-setting and problem-solving techniques, and how faith and spirituality can provide comfort, strength, and meaning in times of struggle. Your mental health challenges—whether depression, anxiety, bipolar disorder, ADHD, or others don't define you. They are part of your story, but not the whole story.

There's no one-size-fits-all approach to mental health, and different resources will resonate with different people. Take the time to explore multiple resources and see which ones are most helpful for you. Remember that seeking help and using resources is a sign of strength, not weakness. You deserve support, and these tools can help guide you through your journey toward healing and wellness. By developing self-awareness, coping strategies, and a strong support system, you are empowering yourself to manage these challenges and live a fulfilling, purposeful life.

Resources

In addition to the tools and strategies outlined in this workbook, having access to helpful resources can provide additional support on your mental health journey. Whether you're seeking professional help, looking for spiritual guidance, or wanting to connect with others who understand what you're going through, there are numerous resources available to help you navigate your mental health challenges.

Here are some valuable resources to consider as you move forward:

1. My websites, social media, and holistic approach to mental health

Website:

www.freedomfromyournarcissist.com

Https://ginatwumasimentalhealth.com

Facebook:

https://www.facebook.com/psychondemand

Instagram:

Https://www.instagram.com/gina_twumasi?igsh=MWJsdWk1
MHhjbjF1NQ%3D%3D&utm_source=qr

TikTok:

https://www.tiktok.com/@ginat38?_t=8dz64I31vgs&_r=1

Podcast:

https://open.spotify.com/episode/6rWZPcwkX9BIFXYaUppW
Ez?si=0JIiIAWxSsWlPB6odbVVnw

Podcast:

https://open.spotify.com/show/0WTA5HHXQmPhWBVm5BAl
Oy?si=yY0P6rxcREiih1RiGKsXDg

YouTube Channel:

https://www.youtube.com/channel/UCfCVXJu6SyCC-
608FwnNxqQ

2. *Online Therapy Platforms & Faith-Based Counseling Services*

If you're looking for professional therapy but aren't sure where to start, online therapy platforms provide access to licensed therapists from the comfort of your home. These platforms can often match you with a therapist based on your specific needs. These services are also for those who want their faith to be a part of their mental health care, faith-based counseling services offer professional therapy with an emphasis on spiritual beliefs and practices.

-Psych On Demand:

-Website: (https://www.ginatwumasimentalhealth.com)

-Offers online counseling from licensed therapists via video, phone, or text chat. Flexible scheduling options are available for teens.

-Do It Afraid:

-Website: (https://www.FreedomFromYourNarcissist.com)

-Provides access to licensed therapists through courses, workbooks, chat, phone, or video sessions. You can communicate with your therapist anytime.

3. *Mental Health Support and Hotlines*

Sometimes, you need immediate help or a safe space to talk when you're feeling overwhelmed. Hotlines, text lines, and online chats can offer you that support in the moment.

-National Suicide Prevention Lifeline:

-1-800-273-TALK (8255)

-Website: [suicidepreventionlifeline.org] (https://suicidepreventionlifeline.org)

- This hotline provides 24/7, free, and confidential support for people in distress.

-Crisis Text Line:

-Text HOME to 741741

-Website: [crisistextline.org] (https://www.crisistextline.org)

-Text-based support for people dealing with a crisis, available 24/7.

-Teen Line:

-Call or text 310-855-4673 or 800-TLC-TEEN (852-8336)

-Website: [teenlineonline.org] (https://teenlineonline.org)

-A teen-to-teen crisis helpline for teenagers needing someone to talk to about mental health challenges, available 6 p.m. to 10 p.m. PST.

4. Read Books and Resources on Mental Health

Sometimes, reading stories, advice, or insights from professionals or others who have been through similar challenges can help you feel less alone and give you new strategies to manage your mental health.

-"You Are Not Broken: Tools to Overcome Trauma & Thrive" by Georgina Twumasi

-"Being Afraid but Freaking Doing It Anyway: Freedom from Your Narcissist!" By Georgina Twumasi

-"The Anxiety and Phobia Workbook" by Edmund J. Bourne

 -A comprehensive resource for people struggling with anxiety, offering strategies and exercises to manage anxiety and panic attacks.

-"The Depression Workbook: A Guide for Living with Depression and Manic Depression" by Mary Ellen Copeland

 -A self-help book that offers practical strategies for managing depression, along with personal stories from individuals living with mood disorders.

-"Borderline Personality Disorder Demystified" by Robert O. Friedel

-A helpful guide that explains Borderline Personality Disorder and provides insights into treatment options and coping mechanisms.

5. Faith and Spirituality Resources

For those who find comfort in their faith, there are many resources that offer spiritual guidance specifically related to mental health challenges. These books, websites, and programs can help you integrate your faith into your healing journey.

-**"Grace for the Afflicted: A Clinical and Biblical Perspective on Mental Illness" by Matthew S. Stanford:**

-A compassionate and well-researched look at mental illness from a Christian perspective, blending scientific understanding with biblical truths.

-**"Anxious for Nothing: Finding Calm in a Chaotic World" by Max Lucado:**

-This book offers Christian wisdom and practical advice for managing anxiety, reminding readers to rely on their faith for peace and comfort.

-**"The Bible and Mental Health" by Dr. John Swinton:**

-A guide that connects mental health challenges with biblical teachings, providing insight into how faith can support emotional well-being.

6. *Support Groups*

Support groups offer a safe space to connect with others who are going through similar struggles. Sharing your experiences in a group setting can provide validation, support, and a sense of belonging.

-National Alliance on Mental Illness (NAMI) Support Groups:

-Website: [nami.org] (https://www.nami.org)

-NAMI offers a wide range of support groups for people living with mental illness and their families. You can find both in-person and online support groups through their website.

-Depression and Bipolar Support Alliance (DBSA) Support Groups:

-Website: [dbsalliance.org] (https://www.dbsalliance.org)

-DBSA offers free, peer-led support groups for individuals living with depression or bipolar disorder. Both online and in-person meetings are available.

-Celebrate Recovery:

-Website: [celebraterecovery.com] (https://www.celebraterecovery.com)

-A Christ-centered recovery program for anyone struggling with addiction, mental health issues, or emotional challenges. Offers community-based support groups.

6. School and Campus Resources

If you're a student, your school may offer mental health resources you can use. Many schools have guidance counselors, mental health professionals, or peer support programs available for students.

-Talk to Your School Counselor or Nurse:

-They can provide mental health referrals, access to mental health professionals, and crisis intervention when needed.

-Join a Mental Health Club or Group:

-Many schools have mental health awareness groups or clubs where students can learn about mental health and support each other.

7. Mental Health Apps

There is many mental health apps designed to help manage anxiety, depression, and stress. These apps offer guided meditation, mood tracking, journaling prompts, and self-care tips. Below are a few to consider:

-Calm:

-Website: [calm.com] (https://www.calm.com)

-Provides guided meditation, breathing exercises, sleep stories, and more to help reduce anxiety and improve sleep.

-Headspace:

-Website: [headspace.com] (https://www.headspace.com)

-A mindfulness and meditation app that offers easy-to-follow meditation exercises designed to reduce stress and improve emotional well-being.

-Moodpath:

-Website: [moodpath.de] (https://www.moodpath.de/en/)

-A mental health app that helps you track your mood, offers insights into your emotional well-being, and provides helpful exercises for managing anxiety and depression.

ANXIETY BREAKTHROUGH BLUEPRINT

BLUEPRINT

Georgina Twumasi

ANXIETY BREAKTHROUGH BLUEPRINT

Welcome to the Anxiety Breakthrough Blueprint, this journal is designed to guide you towards understanding, managing, and embracing your unique relationship with anxiety. Within these pages, you'll embark on a four-week exploration, each week targeting a distinct aspect of anxiety, from its triggers to the intricate dance between our thoughts, emotions, and physical sensations.

This journal is not just about recording experiences—it's a tool to delve deeper, to ask tough questions, and to chart a personalized roadmap towards greater peace and resilience. It's built upon evidence-based approaches and introspective practices that have aided countless individuals in navigating the landscape of anxiety.

The weekly themes will serve as your compass, while daily prompts, affirmations, and exercises will be your stepping stones. Remember, there's no right or wrong way to feel or respond; this is your journey, and every step you take is a testament to your strength and commitment.

Embrace this opportunity with an open heart and mind. Celebrate your progress, no matter how small, and know that with each page, you're forging a deeper understanding and a stronger, more compassionate bond with yourself. Here's to discovery, growth, and the many breakthrough moments that await you.

Georgina Twumasi

DO IT AFRAID
Georgina Twumasi

4wf
4 women's foundation

PSYCH
ON DEMAND

WEEK 1

ANXIETY BREAKTHROUGH BLUEPRINT

_____

IDENTITYING TRIGGERS & COPING MECHANISMS

COMMON TRIGGERS

Understanding and recognizing what sparks our anxiety is the first step towards management; here are 20 common triggers that people frequently encounter.

- *Stressful life events (e.g., moving, job changes)*
- *Health concerns or illness*
- *Certain medications*
- *Excessive caffeine intake*
- *Alcohol consumption and its after-effects*
- *Financial worries or instability*
- *Relationship problems or conflicts*
- *Overcrowded or unfamiliar environments*
- *Loud noises or sudden surprises*
- *Traumatic past experiences*
- *High-pressure work or school situations*
- *Fear of failure or making mistakes*
- *Specific phobias (e.g., spiders, heights)*
- *Public speaking or performances*
- *Lack of sleep or inconsistent sleep patterns*
- *Persistent negative self-talk*
- *Social events or interactions*
- *Personal past experiences that evoke fear*
- *Travel, especially if associated with a fear of flying*
- *Unexpected changes or disruptions in routine*

AIDS & COPING MECHANISMS

Equipping ourselves with a toolbox of strategies can greatly help in navigating the challenges of anxiety; below are 20 effective coping methods to consider.

- *Deep breathing exercises to manage anxiety in social situations*
- *Time management strategies to alleviate work-related stress*
- *Budgeting and financial planning to address money concerns*
- *Communication skills workshops to improve relationships*
- *Mindfulness techniques to navigate sensory overload*
- *Mind mapping to visualize and plan for uncertain situations*
- *Seeking professional counseling for health-related anxieties*
- *Therapeutic writing or art to process past traumas*
- *Active listening techniques for improving communication*
- *Family therapy to address underlying dynamics*
- *Setting media consumption limits for a healthier mindset*
- *Embracing a growth mindset to counteract fear of failure*
- *Joining support groups to connect with like-minded individuals*
- *Affirmations and self-compassion exercises to counter perfectionism*
- *Introducing variety and new experiences to break routine*
- *Cognitive-behavioral techniques to challenge negative self-talk*
- *Setting realistic goals and prioritizing self-care*
- *Grief counseling and memorial activities for healing*
- *Delegating tasks and seeking help to manage responsibilities*
- *Self-esteem boosting exercises to address personal insecurities*

PAIR UP YOUR TRIGGER AND COPING MECHANISM

Trigger   *Aid/Coping Mechanism*

IDEA TO PONDER THIS WEEK

Consider the dance between triggers and coping mechanisms: How might understanding our triggers not as enemies, but as messengers, change the way we respond to them with our coping strategies?

AFFIRMATIONS

Embrace these affirmations as guiding lights for your week; choose the ones that deeply resonate with you and repeat them often, allowing their truth to anchor and empower you in moments of challenge.

Awareness is Power

"With every trigger I recognize, I empower myself to navigate my anxiety with grace and strength."

Growth Through Understanding

"Each moment of anxiety teaches me more about myself, guiding my journey of healing and growth."

Embracing the Process

"I am a work in progress, and every step I take, whether big or small, brings me closer to inner peace."

Compassion Over Criticism
"I choose to treat myself with the same kindness and understanding I'd offer to a loved one facing their triggers."

Journey Over Destination
"Each day I learn and adapt, understanding that managing my anxiety is a journey, not a destination, and I am proud of every step I take."

Strength in Vulnerability
"By acknowledging my triggers, I am not admitting weakness but celebrating my courage to face them head-on."

Choice in Response
"I cannot always control what triggers me, but I always have a choice in how I respond and cope."

ANXIETY CHECK-IN

How would you rate your anxiety level today on a scale from 1 to 10? Where 1 is completely relaxed and 10 is extremely anxious.

1   2   3   4   5   6   7   8   9   10

Exploring Triggers: *Today, when did you feel a surge of anxiety, and what specific event or thought might have triggered it? Was this trigger familiar or new to you?*

Response & Recovery: *How did you respond to anxiety-inducing moments today? Which coping mechanism did you employ, and how quickly did you find yourself returning to a state of calm or balance?*

ANXIETY CHECK-IN

How would you rate your anxiety level today on a scale from 1 to 10? Where 1 is completely relaxed and 10 is extremely anxious.

| 1 | 2 | 3 | 4 | 5 | 6 | 7 | 8 | 9 | 10 |

Exploring Triggers: *Today, when did you feel a surge of anxiety, and what specific event or thought might have triggered it? Was this trigger familiar or new to you?*

Response & Recovery: *How did you respond to anxiety-inducing moments today? Which coping mechanism did you employ, and how quickly did you find yourself returning to a state of calm or balance?*

ANXIETY CHECK-IN

How would you rate your anxiety level today on a scale from 1 to 10? Where 1 is completely relaxed and 10 is extremely anxious.

1   2   3   4   5   6   7   8   9   10

Exploring Triggers: *Today, when did you feel a surge of anxiety, and what specific event or thought might have triggered it? Was this trigger familiar or new to you?*

Response & Recovery: *How did you respond to anxiety-inducing moments today? Which coping mechanism did you employ, and how quickly did you find yourself returning to a state of calm or balance?*

ANXIETY CHECK-IN

How would you rate your anxiety level today on a scale from 1 to 10? Where 1 is completely relaxed and 10 is extremely anxious.

| 1 | 2 | 3 | 4 | 5 | 6 | 7 | 8 | 9 | 10 |

Exploring Triggers: *Today, when did you feel a surge of anxiety, and what specific event or thought might have triggered it? Was this trigger familiar or new to you?*

Response & Recovery: *How did you respond to anxiety-inducing moments today? Which coping mechanism did you employ, and how quickly did you find yourself returning to a state of calm or balance?*

ANXIETY CHECK-IN

How would you rate your anxiety level today on a scale from 1 to 10? Where 1 is completely relaxed and 10 is extremely anxious.

1   2   3   4   5   6   7   8   9   10

Exploring Triggers: *Today, when did you feel a surge of anxiety, and what specific event or thought might have triggered it? Was this trigger familiar or new to you?*

Response & Recovery: *How did you respond to anxiety-inducing moments today? Which coping mechanism did you employ, and how quickly did you find yourself returning to a state of calm or balance?*

SATURDAY

ANXIETY CHECK-IN

How would you rate your anxiety level today on a scale from 1 to 10? Where 1 is completely relaxed and 10 is extremely anxious.

1   2   3   4   5   6   7   8   9   10

Exploring Triggers: Today, when did you feel a surge of anxiety, and what specific event or thought might have triggered it? Was this trigger familiar or new to you?

Response & Recovery: How did you respond to anxiety-inducing moments today? Which coping mechanism did you employ, and how quickly did you find yourself returning to a state of calm or balance?

ANXIETY CHECK-IN

How would you rate your anxiety level today on a scale from 1 to 10? Where 1 is completely relaxed and 10 is extremely anxious.

1   2   3   4   5   6   7   8   9   10

Exploring Triggers: Today, when did you feel a surge of anxiety, and what specific event or thought might have triggered it? Was this trigger familiar or new to you?

Response & Recovery: How did you respond to anxiety-inducing moments today? Which coping mechanism did you employ, and how quickly did you find yourself returning to a state of calm or balance?

ANXIETY NAVIGATOR

Messenger Perspective*: If you were to view your triggers as messengers rather than antagonists, what do you think they might be trying to communicate to you about your needs or boundaries?*

Deep Dive into the Past*: Can you recall a time in your life when a current trigger didn't cause you anxiety? How did your relationship with this trigger evolve over time?*

Strategy Efficacy*: Which coping mechanism felt most natural and effective for you this week? Were there any that didn't resonate or work as well as you'd hoped?*

Compassion Exercise*: Imagine a close friend was experiencing your most prominent trigger. How would you comfort or advise them? Can you extend the same compassion to yourself?*

Anticipatory Coping*: Think about an upcoming event or situation where you might encounter a known trigger. How can you prepare yourself with coping strategies in advance? What might that proactive approach look like?*

WEEK 2

ANXIETY BREAKTHROUGH BLUEPRINT

NAVIGATING THE EMOTIONAL LANDSCAPE

COMMON ANXIETY-RELATED EMOTIONS

Anxiety is a multifaceted emotion, often manifesting in various shades and intensities; below are 20 emotions commonly intertwined with the experience of anxiety.

- *Overwhelm*
- *Fear*
- *Dread*
- *Irritability*
- *Nervousness*
- *Unease*
- *Tension*
- *Worry*
- *Apprehension*
- *Panic*
- *Uncertainty*
- *Agitation*
- *Restlessness*
- *Hopelessness*
- *Insecurity*
- *Frustration*
- *Confusion*
- *Desperation*
- *Helplessness*
- *Paranoia*

EMOTIONAL REGULATION TECHNIQUES

Emotional regulation is about understanding and managing our emotional responses; here are 20 techniques to aid in navigating the complex terrain of our feelings.

- *Deep Breathing: Taking slow, measured breaths to calm the body and mind.*
- *Grounding Techniques: Using the 5-4-3-2-1 method or similar tactics to reconnect with the present.*
- *Mindfulness Meditation: Practicing being present and observing thoughts without judgment.*
- *Progressive Muscle Relaxation: Consciously tensing and then relaxing muscle groups.*
- *Guided Imagery: Picturing a calm, peaceful place or scenario.*
- *Timeout: Taking short breaks when overwhelmed to reset.*
- *Expressive Writing: Journaling feelings and thoughts to process them.*
- *Distraction: Engaging in a different activity to shift focus.*
- *Physical Activity: Exercising to release built-up tension and stress.*
- *Positive Self-talk: Replacing negative thoughts with uplifting affirmations.*
- *Sensory Techniques: Using calming scents, sounds, or textures.*
- *Social Support: Talking to someone trustworthy about feelings.*
- *Problem-solving: Actively seeking solutions to identifiable problems.*
- *Emotion-focused Coping: Acknowledging emotions and finding ways to cope.*
- *Cognitive Reframing: Changing negative thought patterns into positive ones.*
- *Limit Stimulants: Reducing intake of caffeine, sugar, or other stimulants.*
- *Prioritizing Self-care: Setting aside time for activities that rejuvenate the spirit.*
- *Establishing Routine: Maintaining a regular daily schedule.*
- *Setting Boundaries: Clearly defining what is acceptable and saying 'no' when needed.*
- *Seeking Professional Help: Consulting with therapists or counselors.*

PAIR UP YOUR EMOTION AND REGULATION TECHNIQUE

Emotion   *Regulation Technique*

IDEA TO PONDER THIS WEEK

How might our lives transform if we viewed our emotions not as problems to be solved, but as messengers bearing insights into our deepest needs, desires, and boundaries?

AFFIRMATIONS

Embrace the wisdom within these affirmations to guide your emotional journey this week; select those that deeply resonate with your heart, and let their words be a comforting echo during your moments of introspection.

Emotion as Guide

"Every emotion I feel is a guide, teaching me more about myself and my journey."

Power of Reaction

"I am in control of my reactions, even when I cannot control the situation."

Path to Understanding

"By honoring my feelings, I pave the way for deeper understanding and growth."

Worthy of Peace

"I am worthy of peace, and every step I take brings me closer to emotional balance."

Emotional Cartography

"In the vast landscape of my emotions, I am both the traveler and the mapmaker."

Inner Compass

"I trust my inner compass to navigate through my feelings, no matter how stormy they may be."

Strengthening Bonds

"Each day, I cultivate a stronger, more harmonious relationship with my emotions."

ANXIETY CHECK-IN

How would you rate your anxiety level today on a scale from 1 to 10? Where 1 is completely relaxed and 10 is extremely anxious.

1   2   3   4   5   6   7   8   9   10

Emotional Spectrum: Which emotions did you experience today, from the subtlest to the most intense? How did these emotions guide your actions or decisions?

_____

_____

_____

_____

_____

Emotional Response: When you felt a strong emotion today, how did you react initially and how did you wish you had reacted? What regulation technique might help bridge the gap between the two?

_____

_____

_____

_____

_____

_____

ANXIETY CHECK-IN

How would you rate your anxiety level today on a scale from 1 to 10? Where 1 is completely relaxed and 10 is extremely anxious.

1   2   3   4   5   6   7   8   9   10

Emotional Spectrum: Which emotions did you experience today, from the subtlest to the most intense? How did these emotions guide your actions or decisions?

Emotional Response: When you felt a strong emotion today, how did you react initially and how did you wish you had reacted? What regulation technique might help bridge the gap between the two?

ANXIETY CHECK-IN

How would you rate your anxiety level today on a scale from 1 to 10? Where 1 is completely relaxed and 10 is extremely anxious.

| 1 | 2 | 3 | 4 | 5 | 6 | 7 | 8 | 9 | 10 |

Emotional Spectrum: *Which emotions did you experience today, from the subtlest to the most intense? How did these emotions guide your actions or decisions?*

_____

_____

_____

_____

Emotional Response: *When you felt a strong emotion today, how did you react initially and how did you wish you had reacted? What regulation technique might help bridge the gap between the two?*

_____

_____

_____

_____

ANXIETY CHECK-IN

How would you rate your anxiety level today on a scale from 1 to
10? Where 1 is completely relaxed and 10 is extremely anxious.

1   2   3   4   5   6   7   8   9   10

Emotional Spectrum: Which emotions did you experience today, from the subtlest
to the most intense? How did these emotions guide your actions or decisions?

Emotional Response: When you felt a strong emotion today, how did you react
initially and how did you wish you had reacted? What regulation technique might
help bridge the gap between the two?

ANXIETY CHECK-IN

How would you rate your anxiety level today on a scale from 1 to 10? Where 1 is completely relaxed and 10 is extremely anxious.

1   2   3   4   5   6   7   8   9   10

Emotional Spectrum: *Which emotions did you experience today, from the subtlest to the most intense? How did these emotions guide your actions or decisions?*

_____

_____

_____

_____

Emotional Response: *When you felt a strong emotion today, how did you react initially and how did you wish you had reacted? What regulation technique might help bridge the gap between the two?*

_____

_____

_____

_____

_____

_____

ANXIETY CHECK-IN

How would you rate your anxiety level today on a scale from 1 to 10? Where 1 is completely relaxed and 10 is extremely anxious.

| 1 | 2 | 3 | 4 | 5 | 6 | 7 | 8 | 9 | 10 |

Emotional Spectrum: *Which emotions did you experience today, from the subtlest to the most intense? How did these emotions guide your actions or decisions?*

Emotional Response: *When you felt a strong emotion today, how did you react initially and how did you wish you had reacted? What regulation technique might help bridge the gap between the two?*

ANXIETY CHECK-IN

How would you rate your anxiety level today on a scale from 1 to 10? Where 1 is completely relaxed and 10 is extremely anxious.

1   2   3   4   5   6   7   8   9   10

Emotional Spectrum: *Which emotions did you experience today, from the subtlest to the most intense? How did these emotions guide your actions or decisions?*

Emotional Response: *When you felt a strong emotion today, how did you react initially and how did you wish you had reacted? What regulation technique might help bridge the gap between the two?*

ANXIETY NAVIGATOR

Emotional Summary: *Looking back on the week, describe three dominant emotions you felt. How did these emotions influence your interactions, decisions, or overall wellbeing?*

Navigational Mastery: *Which emotional regulation techniques did you find most helpful this week? Were there moments when a specific technique didn't work as expected?*

Insights & Patterns: *Did you notice any patterns or triggers that consistently evoked certain emotions? What insights did you gain about your emotional responses from these patterns?*

Growth Moments: *Recall a challenging emotional moment from this week. How did you handle it, and what would you do differently next time?*

Emotional Vocabulary: *How has your understanding and vocabulary of your own emotions evolved this week? Are there emotions you've become more attuned to or aware of?*

WEEK 3

ANXIETY BREAKTHROUGH BLUEPRINT

COGNITIVE REFRAMING & THOUGHT PATTERNS

COMMON NEGATIVE THOUGHT PATTERNS

Anxiety often stems from deeply ingrained negative thought patterns; below are 20 common distortions that can shape our perceptions and reactions.

- *Catastrophizing: Expecting the worst possible outcome.*
- *Black-and-White Thinking: Seeing things only in extremes with no middle ground.*
- *Overgeneralizing: Making broad conclusions from a single event.*
- *Mind Reading: Assuming you know what others are thinking without evidence.*
- *Fortune Telling: Predicting future events as fact.*
- *Filtering: Focusing only on the negative details while ignoring the positive.*
- *Personalization: Believing you are the cause of external events.*
- *Emotional Reasoning: Believing that because you feel a certain way, it must be true.*
- *Should Statements: Holding yourself to a rigid set of unrealistic expectations.*
- *Labeling: Assigning global negative traits to yourself or others.*
- *Magnifying: Exaggerating the importance of mistakes or fears.*
- *Minimizing: Downplaying positive experiences or achievements.*
- *Blaming: Holding others responsible for your emotions or outcomes.*
- *Jumping to Conclusions: Making assumptions without evidence.*
- *Discounting the Positive: Ignoring or invalidating positive experiences.*
- *Fallacy of Fairness: Feeling resentful because you believe everything should be fair.*

- *Control Fallacies: Believing you're entirely controlled by external forces or that you have control over everything.*
- *Fallacy of Change: Believing someone else should change for you to be happy.*
- *Always Being Right: Unable to admit being wrong.*
- *Heaven's Reward Fallacy: Expecting sacrifice to always be rewarded.*

COGNITIVE BEHAVIORAL TECHNIQUES

Cognitive Behavioral Therapy (CBT) offers a treasure trove of techniques to challenge and shift negative thought patterns; explore 20 of these transformative strategies below.

- *Thought Recording: Keeping a journal of negative thoughts to identify patterns.*
- *Cognitive Restructuring: Challenging and changing irrational beliefs.*
- *Socratic Questioning: Asking deep questions to explore the validity of thoughts.*
- *Behavioral Experiments: Testing the accuracy of negative beliefs in real life.*
- *Graded Exposure: Facing fears in a gradual and controlled manner.*
- *Activity Scheduling: Planning positive activities to counteract negative feelings.*
- *Guided Discovery: Using questions to explore beliefs and their effects.*
- *Pleasure-Predicting Sheet: Predicting the enjoyment of activities and then comparing with actual experience.*
- *Mindfulness Meditation: Practicing presence to distance oneself from negative thoughts.*
- *Role Playing: Enacting scenarios to practice new behaviors and challenge beliefs.*

- *Relaxation Techniques: Deep breathing, progressive muscle relaxation, and visualization.*
- *Positive Data Log: Recording positive experiences to challenge negative beliefs.*
- *Problem Solving: Systematically addressing challenges rather than avoiding them.*
- *Assertiveness Training: Developing the ability to express oneself effectively and stand up for one's rights.*
- *Distraction Techniques: Diverting attention away from negative thoughts.*
- *Reattribution Training: Distributing responsibility where it's due, rather than personalizing everything.*
- *Decatastrophizing: Evaluating the real implications of feared events.*
- *Behavioral Activation: Engaging in activities to counteract depression and negative thoughts.*
- *Self-Monitoring: Observing and recording behaviors to understand their triggers and consequences.*
- *Core Belief Challenge: Identifying and challenging fundamental negative beliefs about oneself.*

PAIR UP YOUR THOUGHT PATTERN AND BEHAVIORAL TECHNIQUE

Negative Thought Pattern   *Cognitive Behavioral Technique*

IDEA TO PONDER THIS WEEK

What if the thoughts we consider as steadfast truths are merely habits of perception, and by recognizing them, we unlock the power to rewrite our own mental narratives?

AFFIRMATIONS

Empower your cognitive journey with the following affirmations; immerse yourself in the ones that resonate deeply, and let them be your guiding mantra throughout the week.

Power of Thought

"My thoughts are tools, and I choose to wield them constructively."

Embracing Change

"I am capable of changing the narrative in my mind to empower my journey."

Trust in Perspective

"Every thought is a perspective, not an absolute truth."

Growth through Awareness

"By recognizing my thought patterns, I pave the way for growth and understanding."

Mindful Mastery

"I am the master of my mind, not the servant to my fleeting thoughts."

Positive Potential

"The power to cultivate positivity lies within my thoughts and actions."

Continuous Evolution

"Each day, I evolve in my understanding and command over my thoughts."

ANXIETY CHECK-IN

How would you rate your anxiety level today on a scale from 1 to 10? Where 1 is completely relaxed and 10 is extremely anxious.

1   2   3   4   5   6   7   8   9   10

Thought Awareness: Which specific thought patterns emerged prominently today, and how did they influence your behavior or mood?

_____

_____

_____

_____

_____

Cognitive Shifts: Did you challenge any negative or unhelpful thoughts today? If so, how did it change the course of your day or the way you felt about a situation?

_____

_____

_____

_____

_____

ANXIETY CHECK-IN

How would you rate your anxiety level today on a scale from 1 to 10? Where 1 is completely relaxed and 10 is extremely anxious.

1   2   3   4   5   6   7   8   9   10

Thought Awareness: Which specific thought patterns emerged prominently today, and how did they influence your behavior or mood?

Cognitive Shifts: Did you challenge any negative or unhelpful thoughts today? If so, how did it change the course of your day or the way you felt about a situation?

ANXIETY CHECK-IN

How would you rate your anxiety level today on a scale from 1 to 10? Where 1 is completely relaxed and 10 is extremely anxious.

1   2   3   4   5   6   7   8   9   10

Thought Awareness: *Which specific thought patterns emerged prominently today, and how did they influence your behavior or mood?*

Cognitive Shifts: *Did you challenge any negative or unhelpful thoughts today? If so, how did it change the course of your day or the way you felt about a situation?*

ANXIETY CHECK-IN

How would you rate your anxiety level today on a scale from 1 to 10? Where 1 is completely relaxed and 10 is extremely anxious.

1   2   3   4   5   6   7   8   9   10

Thought Awareness: *Which specific thought patterns emerged prominently today, and how did they influence your behavior or mood?*

Cognitive Shifts: *Did you challenge any negative or unhelpful thoughts today? If so, how did it change the course of your day or the way you felt about a situation?*

ANXIETY CHECK-IN

How would you rate your anxiety level today on a scale from 1 to 10? Where 1 is completely relaxed and 10 is extremely anxious.

1   2   3   4   5   6   7   8   9   10

Thought Awareness: *Which specific thought patterns emerged prominently today, and how did they influence your behavior or mood?*

Cognitive Shifts: *Did you challenge any negative or unhelpful thoughts today? If so, how did it change the course of your day or the way you felt about a situation?*

ANXIETY CHECK-IN

How would you rate your anxiety level today on a scale from 1 to 10? Where 1 is completely relaxed and 10 is extremely anxious.

1   2   3   4   5   6   7   8   9   10

Thought Awareness: *Which specific thought patterns emerged prominently today, and how did they influence your behavior or mood?*

Cognitive Shifts: *Did you challenge any negative or unhelpful thoughts today? If so, how did it change the course of your day or the way you felt about a situation?*

ANXIETY CHECK-IN

How would you rate your anxiety level today on a scale from 1 to 10? Where 1 is completely relaxed and 10 is extremely anxious.

1   2   3   4   5   6   7   8   9   10

Thought Awareness: *Which specific thought patterns emerged prominently today, and how did they influence your behavior or mood?*

Cognitive Shifts: *Did you challenge any negative or unhelpful thoughts today? If so, how did it change the course of your day or the way you felt about a situation?*

ANXIETY NAVIGATOR

Thought Analysis: *Review the week and identify one recurring negative thought pattern. How did this pattern influence your actions, decisions, or feelings?*

Technique Exploration: *Which Cognitive Behavioral Techniques did you employ this week, and which one resonated the most with you? Why?*

Moments of Mastery: *Recall a situation this week where you successfully challenged or reframed a negative thought. How did it make you feel, and what was the outcome?*

Cognitive Challenges: *Were there moments this week when you felt overwhelmed by your thoughts and found it challenging to apply the techniques? Describe the situation and what you learned.*

Thought Evolution: *How has your understanding and relationship with your thoughts evolved over the past week? Are there specific beliefs or perceptions that have shifted?*

WEEK 4

ANXIETY BREAKTHROUGH BLUEPRINT

IDENTITYING TRIGGERS & COPING MECHANISMS

COMMON PHYSICAL ANXIETY SYMPTOMS

Anxiety not only manifests in the realm of our thoughts and emotions, but it can also produce tangible physical symptoms; here are 20 common physical manifestations to be aware of.

- *Rapid heartbeat or palpitations*
- *Chest pain or discomfort*
- *Shortness of breath*
- *Trembling or shaking*
- *Dry mouth*
- *Sweating excessively*
- *Stomach upset or nausea*
- *Dizziness or lightheadedness*
- *Frequent urination or diarrhea*
- *Fatigue or feeling drained*
- *Muscle tension or aches*
- *Sleep disturbances (insomnia or sleeping too much)*
- *Chills or hot flashes*
- *Numbness or tingling sensations*
- *Tightness in the throat or difficulty swallowing*
- *Feeling restless or agitated*
- *Headaches or migraines*
- *Grinding teeth or jaw pain*
- *Blurred vision*
- *Ringing in the ears (tinnitus)*

MINDFULNESS GROUNDING TECHNIQUES

Grounding in the present moment becomes vital in moments of overwhelming anxiety. Here are 20 mindfulness and grounding techniques designed to pull you back to the here and now.

- *Leaf on a Stream: Visualize your thoughts as leaves floating on water, observing them without judgment.*
- *Heartbeat Meditation: Placing a hand over your heart, feel its beat and rhythm as you breathe.*
- *Temperature Grounding: Hold something cold (like an ice cube) or warm (like a heated cloth) and focus on its sensations.*
- *Sound Mapping: Draw a map of sounds around you, noting their direction and quality.*
- *Weighted Grounding: Using weighted blankets or objects to feel physically anchored.*
- *Mindful Art: Drawing, coloring, or crafting with full attention on the process.*
- *Sensation Naming: Identify and name five things you can feel against your skin at the moment.*
- *Memory Grounding: Recall a favorite memory in vivid detail, using all senses.*
- *Synchronized Movement: Syncing breathing with a simple movement like lifting an arm.*
- *Bubble Visualization: Imagining yourself inside a protective, calming bubble.*
- *Nature Immersion: Mindfully observing plants, trees, or the sky, focusing on the details.*
- *Candle Gazing: Staring at a candle flame, noting its colors, movement, and brightness.*
- *Mindful Stretching: Engaging in slow stretches, focusing on muscle sensations.*

- *Mindful Stretching: Engaging in slow stretches, focusing on muscle sensations.*
- *Touchpoint Grounding: Feeling your feet on the floor or your body in a chair.*
- *Haptic Observation: Focusing on the sensation of an object you're holding without looking.*
- *Mindful Cleaning: Engaging fully in a cleaning task, noting sensations, movements, and results.*
- *Water Grounding: Feeling water run over your hands or taking a mindful shower.*
- *Elevation Visualization: Imagining viewing your surroundings from a bird's-eye view.*
- *Texture Exploration: Touching different fabrics and materials and noting their unique textures.*
- *Aromatic Grounding: Using pleasant scents or essential oils to bring attention to the present.*

PAIR UP YOUR PHYSICAL SYMPTOM AND GROUNDING TECHNIQUE

Phystical Symptom of Anxiety   *Mindfulness Grounding Technique*

IDEA TO PONDER THIS WEEK

How might our physical sensations not only signal our current emotional state but also provide the very tools we need to return to a place of balance and calm?

AFFIRMATIONS

Connect with the powerful relationship between mind and body through these affirmations; select the ones that deeply resonate with you, letting them guide your reflections throughout the week.

Body's Wisdom

"My body holds wisdom, and I am learning to listen and understand its messages."

Present Power

"I ground myself in the present moment, harnessing its peace and clarity."

Physical Reslience

"Each physical sensation is a fleeting moment, reminding me of my body's resilience."

Mind-Body Harmony

"I nourish the connection between my mind and body, recognizing their shared journey."

Sensory Appreciation

"I am grateful for the sensory experiences that connect me to the world around me."

Anchored Strength

"My body is my anchor, grounding me through every challenge and emotion."

Breath's Embrace

"My breath is a sanctuary, embracing and calming me with each inhale and exhale."

ANXIETY CHECK-IN

How would you rate your anxiety level today on a scale from 1 to 10? Where 1 is completely relaxed and 10 is extremely anxious.

| 1 | 2 | 3 | 4 | 5 | 6 | 7 | 8 | 9 | 10 |

Sensory Check-in: *Today, which physical sensation stood out the most to me and what might it be signaling about my emotional or mental state?*

Body's Wisdom: *How did my body support or communicate with me today, and how can I better attune myself to its messages tomorrow?*

ANXIETY CHECK-IN

How would you rate your anxiety level today on a scale from 1 to 10? Where 1 is completely relaxed and 10 is extremely anxious.

1   2   3   4   5   6   7   8   9   10

Sensory Check-in: *Today, which physical sensation stood out the most to me and what might it be signaling about my emotional or mental state?*

Body's Wisdom: *How did my body support or communicate with me today, and how can I better attune myself to its messages tomorrow?*

ANXIETY CHECK-IN

How would you rate your anxiety level today on a scale from 1 to 10? Where 1 is completely relaxed and 10 is extremely anxious.

| 1 | 2 | 3 | 4 | 5 | 6 | 7 | 8 | 9 | 10 |

Sensory Check-in: *Today, which physical sensation stood out the most to me and what might it be signaling about my emotional or mental state?*

Body's Wisdom: *How did my body support or communicate with me today, and how can I better attune myself to its messages tomorrow?*

ANXIETY CHECK-IN

How would you rate your anxiety level today on a scale from 1 to 10? Where 1 is completely relaxed and 10 is extremely anxious.

1   2   3   4   5   6   7   8   9   10

Sensory Check-in: Today, which physical sensation stood out the most to me and what might it be signaling about my emotional or mental state?

Body's Wisdom: How did my body support or communicate with me today, and how can I better attune myself to its messages tomorrow?

ANXIETY CHECK-IN

How would you rate your anxiety level today on a scale from 1 to 10? Where 1 is completely relaxed and 10 is extremely anxious.

1 2 3 4 5 6 7 8 9 10

Sensory Check-in: *Today, which physical sensation stood out the most to me and what might it be signaling about my emotional or mental state?*

Body's Wisdom: *How did my body support or communicate with me today, and how can I better attune myself to its messages tomorrow?*

ANXIETY CHECK-IN

How would you rate your anxiety level today on a scale from 1 to 10? Where 1 is completely relaxed and 10 is extremely anxious.

1   2   3   4   5   6   7   8   9   10

Sensory Check-in: *Today, which physical sensation stood out the most to me and what might it be signaling about my emotional or mental state?*

Body's Wisdom: *How did my body support or communicate with me today, and how can I better attune myself to its messages tomorrow?*

ANXIETY CHECK-IN

How would you rate your anxiety level today on a scale from 1 to 10? Where 1 is completely relaxed and 10 is extremely anxious.

1   2   3   4   5   6   7   8   9   10

Sensory Check-in: *Today, which physical sensation stood out the most to me and what might it be signaling about my emotional or mental state?*

_____

_____

_____

_____

Body's Wisdom: *How did my body support or communicate with me today, and how can I better attune myself to its messages tomorrow?*

_____

_____

_____

_____

ANXIETY NAVIGATOR

Body's Narrative: *Looking back over the week, can I trace a pattern between certain physical sensations and specific emotional triggers or events?*

Mindful Practices: *Which mindfulness or grounding techniques resonated the most with me this week, and why?*

Embracing Moments: *Was there a moment this week when I felt truly connected to my body in a positive way? How can I recreate or extend that feeling?*

Growth and Understanding: *What new insights or understandings about my body's response to anxiety have I gained this week?*

Forward Movement: *Based on this week's reflections, what steps or practices do I want to incorporate into the coming weeks to strengthen my mind-body connection?*

www.ingramcontent.com/pod-product-compliance
Lightning Source LLC
Chambersburg PA
CBHW060231030426
42335CB00014B/1405